INSTITUTE OF LEADERSHIP & MANAGEMENT

SUPERSERIES

Understanding Change

FOURTH EDITION

Published for the
Institute of Leadership & Management by **Pergamon Flexible Learning**

OXFORD   AMSTERDAM   BOSTON   LONDON   NEW YORK   PARIS
SAN DIEGO   SAN FRANCISCO   SINGAPORE   SYDNEY   TOKYO

Pergamon Flexible Learning
An imprint of Elsevier Science
Linacre House, Jordan Hill, Oxford OX2 8DP
200 Wheeler Road, Burlington, MA 01803

First published 1986
Second edition 1991
Third edition 1997
Fourth edition 2003

British Library Cataloguing in Publication Data
A catalogue record for this book is available from the British Library

ISBN 0 7506 5878 9

For information on Pergamon Flexible Learning
visit our website at www.bh.com/pergamonfl

Institute of Leadership & Management
registered office
1 Giltspur Street
London
EC1A 9DD
Telephone 020 7294 3053
www.i-l-m.com
ILM is a part of the City & Guilds Group

The views expressed in this work are those of the authors and do
not necessarily reflect those of the Institute of Leadership &
Management or of the publisher

Author: Jane Edmonds
Editor: Heather Sergeant
Editorial management: Genesys, www.genesys-consultants.com
Based on previous material by Joe Johnson
Composition by Genesis Typesetting Limited, Rochester, Kent
Printed and bound in Great Britain by MPG Books, Bodmin

Contents

Contents

Workbook introduction

1 ILM Super Series study links

This workbook addresses the issues of *Understanding Change*. Should you wish to extend your study to other Super Series workbooks covering related or different subject areas, you will find a comprehensive list at the back of this book.

2 Links to ILM Qualifications

This workbook relates to the following learning outcomes in segments from the ILM Level 3 Introductory Certificate in First Line Management and the Level 3 Certificate in First Line Management.

C4.1   Continuous improvement
1   Recognize the need for achieving continuous improvement
3   Encourage proactivity and positive attitudes to continuous improvement and change

C4.3   Promoting change
1   Communicate and promote plans for change effectively
2   Recognize barriers to change and potential difficulties which may arise during change
3   Identify effective methods for overcoming difficulties
4   Gain the commitment of others, through involvement

C4.5 Forces for change
1 Identify internal and external forces for organizational change
2 Recognize opportunities for own organization created by the forces for changes
3 Recognize threats to the organization from the forces for change

3 Links to S/NVQs in Management

This workbook relates to the following elements of the Management Standards which are used in S/NVQs in Management, as well as a range of other S/NVQs.

A1.3   Make recommendations for improvements in work activities

It will also help you to develop the following Personal Competences:

- building teams;
- communicating;
- focusing on results;
- thinking and taking decisions.

4 Workbook objectives

'Nothing is permanent but change'.

This thought was expressed by Heraclitus, a Greek philosopher living around 500 BC. At the present time in our history, when the rate of change seems to be increasing, the truth behind the above statement is self-evident, particularly when applied to the world of work.

The days when employees did the same job, in the same way, for most of their working lives are long since gone. The working environment has seen many dramatic and far-reaching changes over the last 40 years or so, and it is difficult to imagine that 'the good old days' (if ever they existed!) will return.

Change is not a single hurdle: a problem to be got out of the way before you get back to normal. Change goes on all the time. No organization and no team can afford to stand still: there's no room left for complacency.

A change may be part of a programme of continuous improvement, in which what are often small-scale changes are made to the way things are done, with the ultimate aim of improving the quality of products or services. Or a change may be a one-off, possibly large-scale project, planned by senior management. Either way, you, as a first line manager, are likely to be involved as an instigator of change, as one who encourages others to instigate change, and as one who has to lead and inspire others in implementing change planned by others.

In this workbook we will look at the forces behind change, both in the general environment and within your organization, and the opportunities and threats they can present to both your organization and your team. We will examine the resulting challenges and problems that you and your team will have to confront and look at ways of overcoming the resistance to change that people naturally feel. More than anything else, as a leader of change, you must have the skills necessary to convince others of its benefits – skills that this workbook aims to help you develop.

4.1 Objectives

When you have completed this workbook you will be better able to:

- identify the forces behind change, and how they might affect your organization or department;
- recognize the beneficial aspects of change, whether it be through continuous improvement or through one-off projects;
- take a proactive role, and encourage others to take a proactive role, in initiating change;
- anticipate and recognize reactions to a proposed change, and overcome resistance to the change.

5 Activity planner

The following Activities require some planning so you may want to look at these now.

■ Activities 6, 8 and 11, on pages 10, 13 and 17, ask you – perhaps with the help of your manager and colleagues – to identify factors in the general environment that could act as forces for change within your organization or department.

■ Activity 14, on page 21, asks you – perhaps with the help of your manager and colleagues – to identify your organization's strengths and weaknesses.

■ Activity 34, on page 56, asks you to review a significant change in which you and your team have recently been involved.

Some or all of these Activities may provide the basis of evidence for your S/NVQ portfolio. All Portfolio Activities and the Work-based assignment are posted with this icon.

The icon states the elements to which the Portfolio Activities and Work-based assignment relate.

The Work-based assignment, on page 68, suggests that you discuss with three workteam members or colleagues their experience of change. You might like to start thinking about whom you should approach, and perhaps arrange a time to have a chat with them. This assignment should be useful in helping to demonstrate your competence in:

■ building teams;
■ thinking and taking decisions;
■ influencing others.

Session A
External forces for change

1 Introduction

If, in the 1950s, you had asked someone whether change was unusual – a disruption to the everyday routine – the chances are that they would have said 'yes'. During the 1950s people talked about 'having a steady job', and many jobs followed a predictable routine. Of course, changes did take place – organizations moved premises, people were promoted, new product lines were introduced and so on. But these could be identified as departures from the 'normal' established pattern, to which everyone would return as soon as possible.

The situation today is very different. In all walks of life, in all trades and professions, it is very difficult to define normality. It has become 'normal' to expect regular announcements about the following.

- Mergers and takeovers.
  If we want to keep up with 'who owns whom' we must be keen students of the financial press. (Is your local electricity company now under German control? Or is it part of the same organization that delivers your water?)
- Businesses closing down or opening up.
  These result in many redundancies on the one hand or many new jobs on the other.
- Political and economic changes, affecting millions of people.
  The process of globalization, in which multinational corporations move their operations around the world and individuals travel and communicate with one another across frontiers with ease, means that events in one country can immediately affect people in other countries as never before.
- Technological advances.
  Many – of which the Internet is just one obvious example – promise (or threaten) to make us revise our ways of working.

Nowadays, the only thing you can say with certainty about your job is that it will change!

2

Apart from these large-scale changes, we have to deal with local events that are just as important to us. It doesn't seem helpful to try to identify what is normal because in a very real sense, change is the norm.

2 Categorizing forces for change

Think about almost any aspect of your life – your home, your workplace, where you shop and bank, where you spend your leisure time – and you will be able to identify something that has changed in the last few years.

Activity I · · 5 mins

Identify one change that has occurred in the last few years in each of the following areas.

■ Your home

_____

_____

■ Your workplace

_____

_____

■ Your nearest town

_____

_____

■ The country as a whole

_____

_____

There are, of course, numerous things that you could have written down, depending on your particular situation. But to get an idea of the variety of changes that have occurred, let's consider Janice's situation.

A mother of two teenage children, Janice works as the supervisor of the meat and fish counter in her local supermarket. At home she and her husband have recently bought a high-powered computer in response to the demands of her children, who like to spend many hours each week on the Internet. They have also recently bought a DVD player and a digital TV. Now she and her husband are considering borrowing £8000 to buy a new car because interest rates are so much lower than they were a few years ago. Janice has no financial worries, but she is concerned about her children, one of whom struggles to cope with the growing number of public exams.

At work, Janice is spending more and more time overseeing the packaging of orders for items purchased by customers on-line. She has also had to start looking at new types of fish to order up as stocks of some of the old favourites, such as cod, have diminished and become more expensive. In the past she often drove into town from her house in the suburbs. However, the local council has now created a network of bus and cycle lanes, and made parking much more expensive, so it is easier and cheaper to go by bus. One of the things she regularly enjoys during a shopping trip is a cappuccino in one of the many new coffee bars that have opened up all over town. Always keen on going to the cinema, she now has a wide choice of films every week as two of the local cinemas have become eight-screen complexes.

For her annual holiday she always goes abroad. Flights are so cheap that the whole family has been able to go to Florida twice in the last few years. Whenever she goes away in Britain she is appalled by how much time they spend sitting in traffic jams on the motorway. On the other hand, there are a few resorts on the south coast that she is fond of visiting because they have become 'continental' in feel, with pubs, cafes and restaurants open and selling alcohol all day, and setting up tables and chairs on the pavement. She can remember the time when it was difficult to have a glass of wine in the afternoon because of the licensing laws.

Activity 2 · ⏱ 8 mins

A variety of factors have brought about changes in Janice's life in the last few years. These can be divided into a number of categories, such as political, economic, social, technological, legal or environmental. Try to identify one factor in each category that has brought about change in Janice's life – or the life of her family.

■ Political

_____

_____

■ Economic

_____

_____

■ Social

_____

_____

■ Technological

_____

_____

■ Legal

_____

_____

■ Environmental

_____

_____

To identify political factors that can bring change in your life, you need to consider what new policies have been introduced by the government. In Janice's case, the government's introduction since the 1990s of numerous public exams for children, such as National Curriculum Assessments, is one political factor that has a direct impact on her family's life.

A major economic factor that has affected Janice's life is the drop in interest rates. Social factors include various changes in the leisure sector, such as cinemas becoming multi-screen complexes and an increasing number of coffee bars serving up Italian-style coffee. Technological factors include the ever-changing capabilities of personal computers and the introduction of digital TV. Legal factors include various changes in the licensing laws, which from 1988 allowed all-day opening of pubs in England and Wales and made it possible to buy an alcoholic drink any time of the day.

Finally, there are the environmental factors. For Janice, these include the introduction of bus and cycle lanes in an attempt by the local council to cut down on pollution by cars. There is also the fact that over-fishing has had a major impact on stocks of popular fish such as cod, causing the European Commission to impose strict quotas and forcing retailers to find other fish to sell – so bringing about change in Janice's job.

All the factors that have caused change in Janice's life will have had an effect on various organizations, from exam boards to bus companies, supermarkets, pubs, restaurants, cinema chains, and so on. If such organizations do not make a point of scanning the general environment for changes that could well have an impact on them, their business will ultimately suffer. As a manager you can play a part in identifying these external forces for change – and become aware of developments that may have an effect on your job and the jobs of your team – by carrying out what is known as a PESTLE analysis. (PESTLE is an acronym derived from the words: political, economic, social, technological, legal and environmental.)

It's worth bearing in mind that it's not always easy to isolate one type of factor from another – many political factors are also economic, for example. And, in fact, this doesn't really matter. The main purpose of doing a PESTLE analysis is to get you thinking about what is happening in the external environment, and what changes you, your team and your organization should consider making in response.

Activity 3 · 10 mins

Read through the following two examples of change. As you read them make a note of the types of factors that brought about the change. Were they political, economic, social, technological, legal or environmental? Briefly explain the reasons for your answer in each case.

Example 1

Caroline Quigley has been a clerk at the old-established firm of Terence Gratton Ltd for more than twenty years. Until about ten years ago, she would have described her job as 'mostly paperwork'. Then the company computerized nearly all clerical functions, and Caroline had to learn to work at a keyboard, and to produce results using a complex customized accounting package. It was a difficult period of adjustment, but now she couldn't imagine going back to the old ways.

However, as Caroline had discovered, it wasn't a simple question of learning a set of procedures and putting them into practice. The organization has been branching into new areas of business and its customer base is continuously changing. In addition, the software company that provided the computer package is regularly updating the system and the equipment has already been upgraded three times.

When she thinks about it, Caroline is surprised by how well she has coped with it all. She had once been 'computer illiterate', but others in the office now look to her for expert help.

Example 2

Robertson's was the only second-hand bookshop in the Highfields area of Busbury and brought its owner, Tom, a steady but unspectacular income. When another second-hand bookshop opened up just down the road, Tom wasn't worried at first as he felt his shop had many unique features that would continue to attract the customers. He was well-known for his large sections on the cinema, theatre and art. Furthermore, he was always being told by customers how much they appreciated the detailed knowledge he and his assistant had of their stock. Several customers had actually written to say that they had been delighted that he had managed to track down a particular book they wanted at another bookseller's.

Unfortunately for Tom, his competitor down the road, Meera, had taken a good look at Robertson's and come to the conclusion that while Robertson's had a really good selection, many of the books were over-priced. The thing to do was to set up a bargain section in which books were offered at prices that undercut those at Robertson's. Meera was also well aware that many second-hand bookshops were beginning to struggle as a result of competition from dealers selling books on the Internet. She decided that the best way to cope with this was to acquire a computer herself and start selling her more valuable books on the Internet herself. She already had some basic computer skills – she just needed to brush up on creating a database. Once she had got her toe in the market using a Website with which many bookshops were registered, she might even consider setting up her own Website.

Much as Tom's customers appreciated the service they got in his shop, many of them appreciated Meera's prices even more. However, Meera doubted if this would have been enough to keep her in business if she had not decided to start selling on the Internet. She entered titles in the database whenever she had a spare moment, and she was amazed at how her sales began to increase dramatically, Every day Tom saw her setting off to the post office with a pile of parcels to send to customers while he fretted over his declining till receipts. She had told him about her success with the Internet but he didn't see how he could follow suit as he and his assistant knew nothing about computers. Within a year Tom' shop was doing only half the trade it had before. Increasingly demoralized by the lack of customers, and approaching an age when he could retire, he decided that he had no alternative but to close down.

Example 1

Change factors

_____

Reasons for answer

_____

_____

Example 2

Change factors

_____

Reasons for answer

_____

_____

So what conclusions did you come to about the types of factors that produced change in the two examples? In Caroline Quigley's case, there was certainly technology involved, as computerization only comes through advances in technology. But the investment in technology was part of the company's efforts to stay efficient, and to keep up with a changing marketplace. You might have decided that the root cause of the changes was an economic one.

In Tom Robertson's case, the closure of the shop seems to have been brought about by competition, which is an economic force. But there were social and technological forces at work, too. His competitor, Meera, doubted whether she could have stayed in business without her Internet sales. The demand among local customers for ordinary second-hand books seemed to be going down at the same time as the Internet made it possible to sell the rarer and more valuable books to customers throughout the world.

As even these two examples show, more than one factor is generally at work in creating the need for change. And in the case of businesses that have to make a profit, one of these factors will almost certainly be economic.

3 Political, economic and social factors

Unless you keep up-to-date with the news, you may not always be aware of many political, economic and social developments. All can have a major impact on you and your team.

3.1 Political factors

The government in power, and the policies that the government pursues, can have a major impact on organizations. A government decision, for example, to have low inflation as a chief goal results in interest rates being set low, which in turn means that people are happy to borrow more and spend more in the shops. They are also prepared to spend a lot more on housing, which means an increase in business for estate agents, banks and building societies.

Returning to the example of increasing the number of public examinations for school children: by 2002 children had up to 87 official tests in their school careers. As a result, there has been a huge expansion of business for the organizations responsible for the setting and marking of examination papers – all the result of political changes.

3.2 Economic factors

Some developments in the economy are dictated by government policies, notably measures announced in the annual budget, such as a cut in corporation tax for small businesses, or an increase in employers' national insurance contributions.

Other economic developments have nothing to do with the government. The destruction of New York's World Trade Centre on 11 September 2001 by two planes that had been hijacked by terrorists had major worldwide effects. One example was the downturn in the demand for airline tickets. This, in turn, meant that a few airlines, such as Swissair, actually went out of business, while others, such as British Airways, had to reduce the number of flights and routes on which they operated as their profits slumped in the period that followed.

Quite apart from economic pressures created by governments and world events, there are those to which most organizations have to react in the course of a year.

Activity 4   4 mins

Jot down two or three economic pressures to which most organizations may have to react in the course of a year.

_____

_____

_____

_____

_____

You could have listed the following:

- the pressure of competition – to compete with their rivals, companies have to try to make their products or services more attractive in some way, so as to retain or increase their share of the market;
- pressure from shareholders, who demand high profits and dividends;
- pressure from financial institutions, who lend the money organizations need for investment, but who demand interest and prompt payment.

3.3 Social factors

Social factors may be long-term or fleeting. Among long-term factors are changes in the age profile and ethnic composition of the population. As people live longer, the percentage of people over the age of 50 is increasing considerably, and more and more businesses are now considering how to address their needs. This particularly applies to people who have retired early, have a good pension and lots of leisure time.

Among the more fleeting social factors are fashions in clothes. What has been popular in the past is no indicator of what people will buy in the future. The shape of jeans or the length of skirts, for example, changes from year to year.

Activity 5

What other short-term social changes can you think of, apart from fashions in clothes? Jot down two or three.

_____

_____

_____

Look at a guide to TV programmes for the coming week and you'll be able to spot areas in which short-term change is the norm. You will probably find lots of programmes about house décor, revealing what colours, materials and styles of furniture are fashionable. Food and wine is also a common subject. Sun-dried tomatoes, goats' cheese, rocket salad and chardonnay wines all became popular items in bistro-style restaurants in the 1990s. What items will replace them in the next decade? There has also been a massive increase in the number of programmes in which groups of people are brought together in sometimes difficult situations and are then the subject of constant filming. 'Big Brother' is a famous example, but there have been many others. You have probably thought of many other forms of entertainment that have changed considerably in the last decade.

Activity 6

S/NVQ A1.3

This Activity may provide the basis of appropriate evidence for your S/NVQ portfolio. If you are intending to take this course of action, it might be better to write your answer on separate sheets of paper.

Are there any political, economic and social factors that you think your organization or, if you work for a large organization, your department should take account of in the near future? (You may find it helpful to talk to your manager and colleagues about this.) Note down what they are and what effect they could have on your organization if it did not make any changes in response to these factors.

Political factors

_____

_____

Possible effects

_____

_____

Economic factors

_____

_____

Possible effects

_____

_____

Social factors

_____

_____

Possible effects

_____

_____

You may have found this Activity quite difficult. If so, you should think about ways in which you can keep up-to-date with the full range of developments that may affect your organization or department in the future. These include:

- reading journals and newspapers;
- talking to suppliers' representatives;
- reading company newsletters and bulletins;
- attending management briefings;
- going on relevant courses;
- talking to colleagues in other parts of the organization, and in other organizations.

4 Technological factors

A great many changes that take place at work are driven by developments in technology. If we go back in history, the most fundamental change in working life in Britain came about as a result of the invention of machines such as the spinning jenny and the steam engine in the second half of the eighteenth century. Before this Industrial Revolution, most people worked on the land or in cottage industries – in 1750, only about 20% of England's population lived in towns. After this date there was a vast increase in the number of people toiling in factories and coalfields and by 1850 over 50% lived in towns.

Now we seem to be coming full circle, as many more of the population are working from home or in small businesses. Technology is a major factor in the change. The post-industrial revolution is with us: only about 20% of workers in Britain are employed by manufacturing companies, and most coal mines have been closed.

But who can say whether this will be the picture in 20 or 30 years' time?

Activity 7

3 mins

Apart from the computer, what inventions in the 20th and 21st centuries have changed, or are in the process of changing, the way people work? Jot down two or three.

_____

_____

_____

You might have mentioned:

■ various forms of transport, such as cars, aeroplanes and high-speed trains;
■ space technology;

- modern telecommunications, including permanent and mobile phones, and satellite links;
- the Internet;
- automation and industrial robots;
- modern fabrics;

or a hundred other inventions.

It is clear that technology is changing all our lives and promises to alter them even more in the future.

Activity 8

5 mins

Portfolio of evidence

S/NVQ A1.3

This Activity may provide the basis of appropriate evidence for your S/NVQ portfolio. If you are intending to take this course of action, it might be better to write your answer on separate sheets of paper.

Make a note of two or more ways in which you anticipate your job, and the jobs of your team, may be changed within the next few years as a result of new technological changes. (You may find it helpful to talk to your manager and colleagues about this.)

_____

_____

_____

_____

_____

We can all speculate about what might happen in the future, but it is more useful is to base your predictions on known facts. For example, if you use plastics, are you aware of developments in the chemical industry, where new kinds of plastics are being tested? Or if you work in building, you may have heard about new materials or processes, which may outdate existing practices. Most kinds of work are likely to change in the future as a result of new technology.

Remember: wise managers make it their business to keep a close watch on changing events in their own industry, whatever the causes.

5 Legal factors

Laws and regulations affect employment in many ways. For example, the law has brought about changes, generally for the better, in working practices. In 1842, a law was passed forbidding the employment of children under ten years of age in coal mines. At that time workers had virtually no rights. Today the working population is protected in a number of ways, through a series of Acts of Parliament.

This is one area of law – employee protection law.

Other kinds of law which affect the workplace include:

- health and safety law;
- laws governing the conduct of unions;
- contract law;
- insurance law;
- consumer protection law;
- laws controlling the carriage of goods;
- company law, which deals with the registration of companies and the auditing of company finances.

Activity 9

3 mins

Can you think of any laws or regulations in the last decade or so that have forced organizations to introduce change – either in the way they treat their staff, in the processes they employ, or in the products or services they provide? Jot down a couple of examples.

One comparatively recent example of a law that has affected conditions for staff is the introduction of the minimum wage in 1999. Before its introduction many organizations protested about it and said that it would cause job losses and even put some of them out of business. In fact, it had none of the feared effects.

As far as products are concerned, among the legal measures that have produced change are those banning the use of leaded petrol (in 2000) and the use of ozone-depleting chlorofluorocarbons (CFCs) in fridges and aerosols (in 1995). Both reflect a growing concern with the effect we are having on the environment. This brings us to the next set of factors that contribute to change.

6 Environmental factors

Scientists don't all agree about many questions on the environment. But you don't have to be a 'green' to admit that there has been a significant change in public awareness of these issues.

Since the 1980s there has been ever-increasing concern about the effect of human activities on the environment. There are two main environmental issues.

■ The Earth and its atmosphere do not have an unlimited capacity to cope with the many forms of pollution associated with industrialization.
■ The Earth does not have unlimited resources for the world's population to exploit and destroy.

6.1 Pollution

Industrial pollution has been a problem in Britain since the 19th century. The terrible smogs that engulfed London in 1952, killing hundreds, showed just how much damage could be done by pollution. In this case the pollution was caused by smoke from burning coal.

It's now known that one of the effects of atmospheric pollution is the depletion of the ozone layer. This layer of ozone filters the sun's rays, and protects us from over-exposure to the ultra-violet radiation. If the layer were to disappear completely we would all be dead. Its loss is blamed on substances produced by industrial processes. Chemicals called chlorofluorocarbons

(CFCs), traditionally used in refrigerators and aerosols, have been identified as being partly to blame. It has been proved that CFCs react in the atmosphere with ultra-violet radiation to form chlorine. This results in the ozone being converted to oxygen. Governments and manufacturers have been forced to respond to this threat. In many countries there has been a ban since 1995 on the use of CFCs in the production of goods – though there are still many old fridges around containing CFCs.

Another major environmental problem that you will have heard about is global warming. A layer of carbon dioxide in the Earth's atmosphere traps heat from the sun's rays in a naturally occurring process known as the 'greenhouse effect'. It is now generally believed that this greenhouse effect has been increased by the emission of carbon dioxide from the burning of fossil fuels, such as coal and oil, leading to a rise in the Earth's average temperature. The effect could be the melting of ice throughout the world, a rise in the level of the world's oceans, and the flooding of low-lying areas. Governments have responded by attempting to reach agreement on cutting carbon dioxide emissions. This has affected many industries. In Britain, for example, gas has largely replaced coal as the fuel burnt in the production of electricity, and there are now very few coal mines still operating.

6.2 Finite resources

Contributing to the increase in the amount of carbon dioxide in the atmosphere is the destruction of the world's forests. Trees (which absorb carbon dioxide) are among the Earth's finite resources and there is an ongoing campaign in many countries to stop them disappearing. There is also a campaign to stop the extinction of many species of plants and animals. It would be hard to imagine 50 years ago that cod would one day be in danger of becoming extinct as a result of over-fishing.

A development that represents a threat to some organizations can represent an opportunity to others.

Hand-in-hand with efforts to stop the dangerous depletion of various resources and to cut down on the amount of pollution are efforts to recycle as much as possible. All organizations in Britain now have to abide by regulations on the production and recycling of waste. Others have taken advantage of the public's concern over what we are doing to the environment and now produce goods that use natural resources. They may also be sold in recyclable packaging. The Body Shop and its competitors, such as Aveda and Origins, are obvious examples.

The success of businesses such as The Body Shop reflects growing public concern over what we are doing to the environment. This concern is reflected in the products and services that some organizations offer.

Activity 10 · 4 mins

In your local shops or supermarket you will almost certainly find a number of products that reflect public concern with environmental issues. Write down the names of two or three of these products and how they reflect this concern.

_____

_____

_____

Most supermarkets now sell organic products in response to growing unease about the effect modern farming techniques are having on the land, on animals, and on our health. The campaign against genetically modified (GM) foods, and the refusal of many people to buy them, also partly reflects concern about the effects of GM crops on the natural environment. The problem of CFCs has resulted in sprays that are CFC-free and in cleaning products with ingredients that will not harm the environment.

There are many other examples that you may have thought of.

Activity 11 · 10 mins

S/NVQ A1.3

This Activity may provide the basis of appropriate evidence for your S/NVQ portfolio. If you are intending to take this course of action, it might be better to write your answer on separate sheets of paper.

Are there any legal and/or environmental factors that you think your organization or department should take account of in the near future? What are they and what effect they could have on your organization if it did not make any changes in response to these factors? (Again you may find it helpful to talk to your manager and colleagues about this.)

_____

_____

_____

_____

_____

7 Recognizing opportunities and threats

You may remember that in Section 3 we considered the example of Tom Robertson's second-hand bookshop. The business came under threat when another bookshop opened up down the road selling many titles at lower prices than those charged by Tom. Tom's rival, Meera, then increased her profits and made her position more secure by starting to sell her more valuable books on the Internet. Tom's response was eventually to give up and go out of business. But Tom could have decided to seize his opportunities and actually compete. He, too, could have used the Web to sell his more valuable books. He had an excellent stock so there was a good chance that taking this route could have saved his business.

A particular set of changes in the external environment can represent both threats and opportunities for an organization. Ovaltine, a malt and egg powder drink stopped being manufactured in Britain in 2002. Marketed as a drink that is both good for you and helps to put you to sleep, it lost its appeal in a society where people lead increasingly busy lives and want drinks and snacks to keep them going rather than knock them out. Ironically, the original Swiss version of Ovaltine was renowned for its ability to increase energy and was the official drink at the 1948 Olympics. But the manufacturers of Ovaltine failed to capitalize on this while other soft drink manufacturers, such as Lucozade, responded to the growing demand for drinks that give energy and can act as an indispensable aid for anyone doing a sport.

Activity 12 · 5 mins

S/NVQ A1.3

This Activity may provide the basis of appropriate evidence for your S/NVQ portfolio. If you are intending to take this course of action, it might be better to write your answer on separate sheets of paper.

Look back at Activities 6, 8 and 11, in which you identified a range of factors that might have an effect on your organization or department. Do any of these represent threats to your organization? Do any represent opportunities? (Remember the same factors can be both threats and opportunities.) Make a note of any opportunities and threats that you identify.

Opportunities

_____

_____

Threats

_____

_____

8 Strengths and weaknesses

Whether your, or any other organization, is actually capable of responding to the threats and taking advantage of the opportunities will depend on its strengths and weaknesses.

These will include:

- the things it does well or badly;
- its resources or lack of them in certain areas;
- its staff skills or gaps in these skills;
- the high or low staff morale;
- the high or low demand for its products or services;
- its strong or weak financial situation.

Activity 13

Returning to the example of Tom Robertson's bookshop, on the basis of the information you've received so far, what would you say were its main strengths and weaknesses?

Strengths

_____

_____

_____

Weaknesses

_____

_____

_____

Among the strengths of Tom Robertson's bookshop were its large, well-organized sections on subjects, such as cinema, theatre and art, not covered in much depth by rival bookshops. Tom and his assistant also had a detailed knowledge of their stock and were always more than willing to help customers find the book they want. If they didn't have it themselves they would discover a bookseller somewhere in the country who did.

On the other hand, the business had several weaknesses. Tom generally over priced the more ordinary second-hand books. He and his assistant were feeling increasingly demoralized by the lack of customers on some days. In fact, there were some weeks when the shop barely took enough to cover all the outgoings. They had heard about the success of their rival down the road in doing business on the Internet, but neither of them had any computer skills.

Activity 14

10 mins

S/NVQ A1.3

This Activity may provide the basis of appropriate evidence for your S/NVQ portfolio. If you are intending to take this course of action, it might be better to write your answer on separate sheets of paper.

You might find it helpful to discuss the questions in this Activity with your manager and colleagues.

What are your organization's or department's strengths? Consider the following questions and jot down any strengths you can identify below.

- What does it do well?
- What resources does it have?
- What skills do its staff have?
- Is staff morale high?
- Is there a high demand for its products or services?
- Is it in a strong financial situation?

_____

_____

_____

_____

What are your organization's or department's weaknesses? Consider the following questions and jot down any weaknesses you can identify below.

- What does it do badly?
- What resources does it lack?
- What are the gaps in the skills of its staff?
- Is staff morale low?
- Is there only a low demand for its products or services?
- Is it in a weak financial situation?

_____

_____

_____

_____

9 Putting it all together: SWOT analysis

In identifying your organization's strengths and weaknesses, and the opportunities and threats presented by the external environment, you have in effect carried out what is called a **SWOT** analysis. This can act as a springboard for change, helping managers to understand the nature of the organization they are working for and identify ways of moving forward in the future.

A SWOT analysis is usually set out in a box divided into four sections, as in the example below.

SWOT analysis for Tom Robertson's Bookshop

Strengths	Weaknesses
■ Well-organized and extensive sections on cinema, theatre and art ■ Staff have detailed knowledge of stock ■ Able and willing to locate books held by other book-sellers	■ Ordinary books perhaps priced too high ■ Demoralized staff ■ Staff lack computer skills ■ Low and declining profits/little capital
Opportunities	**Threats**
■ Can sell more valuable books on Internet	■ Nearby competitor selling books at lower prices ■ Declining market for ordinary second-hand books

Looking at this SWOT analysis it is clear that Tom Robertson needed to start capitalizing on his excellent sections on cinema, theatre and art, and start selling on the Internet. It is also clear that there were various weaknesses he should have addressed, such as the prices of his ordinary books and his, and his assistant's, lack of computer skills. Although he had little capital, he could have considered borrowing enough to buy a computer and pay for a computer skills course. This would have been a major change for Tom, but was necessary if he was to stay in business.

Activity 15 · 10 mins

S/NVQ A1.3

This Activity may provide the basis of appropriate evidence for your S/NVQ portfolio. If you are intending to take this course of action, it might be better to write your answer on separate sheets of paper.

Try doing a SWOT analysis for your organization or department. As preparation, first look over your answers to Activities 12 and 14.

Strengths	Weaknesses
Opportunities	**Threats**

Once you have done a SWOT analysis you may be able to make some suggestions on what changes your organization can make to:

■ build on its strengths;
■ rectify its weaknesses;
■ grasp opportunities;
■ overcome threats.

Activity 16 · 8 mins

S/NVQ A1.3

This Activity may provide the basis of appropriate evidence for your S/NVQ portfolio. If you are intending to take this course of action, it might be better to write your answer on separate sheets of paper.

Looking at your SWOT analysis, what suggestions do you have for change in your organization or department?

_____

_____

_____

_____

Scanning the general environment outside your organization will at least enable you to keep abreast of developments so you won't be taken by surprise when they lead to change for you and your team. Better still, it may give you ideas on new directions or new ways of doing things for your team, and so help you to have a proactive role in change.

Self-assessment 1

15 mins

1 What categories of factors that can act as forces for change does PESTLE stand for? Put a tick against the correct answer.

a Political, Ethical, Social, Technological, Legal and Environmental

b Political, Economic, Social, Technological, Legal and Ethical

c Political, Economic, Social, Technological, Legal and Environmental

d Political, Economic, Social, Technological, Legal and Epidemiological

2 Complete each of the following sentences with one of the words from the PESTLE acronym.

a Pressures created by financial institutions, as well as governments and world events, contribute to _____ factors.

b _____ factors may be long-term or fleeting. Among the long-term factors are changes in the composition of the population.

c The policies pursued by government help to shape _____ factors.

d Consumer protection laws are among the _____ factors.

e Among _____ factors is the issue of finite resources.

f Numerous inventions that have changed the way people work are among the _____ factors.

3 Fill each of the gaps in the following sentences with one of the words from the SWOT acronym.

Among an organization's _____ are the things it does well and the skills of its staff. Among an organization's _____ are the gaps in staff skills. _____ are those things in the environment that an organization must overcome. _____ are those things an organization should grasp if it is to develop and prosper.

4 As a manager you need to keep up-to-date with developments that may affect your organization in the future. Name three ways in which you can do this.

_____

_____

_____

5 Which of the following two sentences do you think is most correct? Briefly explain the reason for your choice.

a Increasing concern about environmental issues can only represent a threat to organizations.

b Increasing concern about environmental issues can represent an opportunity for some organizations.

The most correct statement is _____ because:

_____

_____

_____

Answers to these questions can be found on page 78.

10 Summary

- Nowadays change is not a disruption of normality: in a very real sense, change is the norm.

- Forces in the general environment that lead to change in organizations can be categorized as:
  - Political factors
  - Economic factors
  - Social factors
  - Technological factors
  - Legal factors
  - Environmental factors

- Carrying out a PESTLE analysis will help you to identify the external forces for change that may affect your organization and your department in the future.

- You can keep up-to-date with developments that may affect your department by:
  - reading journals and newspapers;
  - talking to suppliers' representatives;
  - reading company newsletters and bulletins;
  - attending management briefings;
  - going on relevant courses;
  - talking to colleagues in your own and other organizations.

- By carrying out a SWOT analysis for an organization (or department) you identify the following.
  - Strengths
  - Weaknesses
  - Opportunities
  - Threats

- An organization's strengths and weaknesses are internal factors. They include:
  - the things it does well or badly;
  - its resources or lack of them in certain areas;
  - its staff skills or gaps in these skills;
  - the high or low staff morale;
  - the high or low demand for its products or services;
  - its strong or weak financial position.

- The opportunities and threats are presented by the external environment.

- Carrying out a SWOT analysis should enable you to identify ways in which an organization, or department, can:
  - build on its strengths;
  - rectify its weaknesses;
  - grasp opportunities;
  - overcome threats.

Session B
Continuous improvement and change

1 Introduction

In the last session you identified some changes that your organization might make in response to a range of external factors. It's almost certain that among these external factors will be particular needs and wants of customers – both actual and potential. If Tom Robertson (our bookseller from Session A) had started to sell his books on the Internet, he would have been responding to the need of customers to be able to order rare second-hand books from booksellers anywhere in the world.

In many ways Tom Robertson offered a quality service to his customers. For example, he was always happy to find any book they wanted, whether it be in his shop or with another bookseller. And yet his business declined, at least partly because the prices he was charging were too high compared with those of his main competitor. He had not understood that providing a quality service or product means meeting the needs of customers at prices they can afford.

In today's highly competitive world, even this does not necessarily guarantee that an organization will succeed. It should aim to go further than this and continuously improve its products and services so that they meet, and eventually exceed, customer needs.

Continuous improvement means constant, but also gradual, change, as you will see in this session.

2 Quality and continuous improvement

The idea that organizations should aim to improve the quality of their products and services on a continuous basis was first taken up in Japan. During the period of post-war reconstruction in the 1950s, manufacturing industries in Japan drew on the ideas of the American, W. Edwards Deming. He argued that if an organization improved the quality of its products during the production process, costs would decrease because there would be less need for reworking. The combination of better quality and lower prices would result in an increase in the number of customers, so enabling the organization to expand and flourish.

Improvements in processes were essential to improvements in the quality of products and services. And the way to improve processes was not to rely on managers to come up with all the ideas on how this might be done, but to encourage all staff to make suggestions. The theory was that they should be encouraged to do this on a continuous basis.

Japanese companies, such as Nikon, Toyota and Sony, that adopted the ideas of Deming became known for the superior quality and reliability of their products and were extremely successful from the 1960s onwards. The quality movement spread to other parts of the world and today numerous organizations in the UK aim to deliver high-quality products and services.

So what does continuous improvement – or *kaizen*, as it is called in Japan – mean in practice?

2.1 Continuous improvement cycle

A useful model to follow in planning a programme of continuous improvement is the cycle, shown in the diagram below. It consists of:

- doing;
- reviewing what has been done;
- learning from this review;
- planning improvements on the basis of what you have learnt;
- implementing the improvements;
- reviewing and learning from this, and so on.

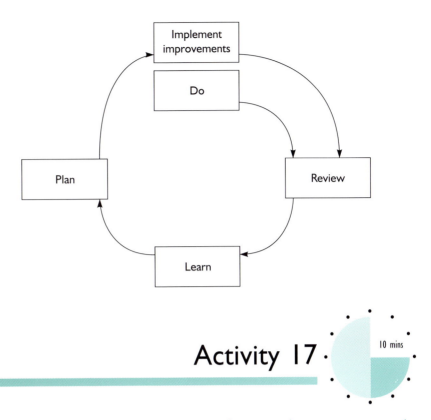

Activity 17

10 mins

Below is an example of how one small incident caused a manager to use the continuous improvement cycle.

Pete is the new manager of the repro department for a printer that specializes in printing brochures and leaflets cheaply and quickly. He and his staff are responsible for 'repro', which means that they take artwork usually sent to them on disks by designers and from it produce film and then plates. One day he receives a telephone call that makes his heart sink: a client has just received proofs for a leaflet that is due to be printed that evening, in time for a conference in two days' time, and there are two mistakes on the cover, which will have to be put right. A block of text is in completely the wrong typeface and one of the pictures is missing. Correcting these mistakes is not only going to take up precious time but is also going to be costly as the printing plates will have to be remade.

How, Pete wonders, could this have happened? Why had they got almost to the point of printing the leaflet before anyone spotted the mistake? What was wrong with the processes followed by his staff – or the designer who had supplied the artwork in the first place? The first thing to do was to compare a copy of the proof with the print-out provided by the designers. This revealed that everything was as it should be on the designer's print-out, so why hadn't anyone spotted there was a problem when they produced the film that was then used to make the plates? It turned out that in their hurry to get the job done, nobody had checked the film against the print-out. If they had checked the film they would have discovered they had a problem – almost certainly because the designers had not supplied all the type fonts and images that were being used in the job. As it was, Pete was going to have to get back to the designers and get them to re-supply the artwork, thus losing valuable time. They were going to be lucky to meet the deadline for getting the leaflets printed.

It was only by paying two members of staff to do some overtime and work well into the night that Pete was able to get the leaflet printed and delivered in time for the client's conference. Once the panic was over he decided it was time to improve not only the processes followed by his staff but also those followed by the designers who supplied them with artwork. His plan was to produce:

■ a checklist for designers on what must be present when supplying artwork on a disk, such as all necessary type fonts and images;

■ a form for his staff listing what should be checked and signed off at each stage, which included the checking of film against the designer's print-out prior to making plates.

The checklist and form were produced and distributed. Over the next few weeks, Pete made a point of checking the forms he had given to staff to see that they were comparing film with designers' print-outs as a matter of course. He also asked the staff to help him in checking to see whether all designers were now supplying everything that was required of them and soon discovered that two of them were still getting things wrong, particularly when deadlines were tight. This was resulting in problems for everyone involved, so Pete was determined to find a way of improving the situation. He decided to send a letter to all designers, advising them to invest in some software that would automatically report on any technical faults and imperfections in a piece of artwork, and collect all the fonts and images used in the artwork.

Pete knew that this probably wouldn't be the end of the problem and that he would have to keep on reviewing the situation, but he was confident that he was on the way to not only providing a quality service to the printer's clients but also receiving a quality service from his suppliers.

■ What does the manager learn as a result of reviewing a process?

_____

_____

■ What does he or she then plan and do?

_____

_____

■ What does he or she learn as a result of an ongoing review?

_____

_____

■ What does he or she then plan and do the second time round?

_____

_____

In reviewing the processes involved in repro, Pete learnt that designers were not always supplying high-quality artwork in which all the necessary components were present, and that his own staff were not always making the necessary checks of film against designers' print-outs. He then planned to improve the process employed by both his staff and designers by preparing a checklist and form, both of which were produced and distributed. His ongoing review then revealed that two designers were still not doing all that was required of them, and so he planned to send them a letter advising them to invest in some software that would help considerably.

2.2 Being proactive in change

When things go wrong at work, it's easy to blame the staff involved. But in fact the great majority of problems are caused by defects in systems and processes.

One of the things you may have noticed in reading about Pete and the repro department is that he focused on getting processes right rather than criticizing people for their mistakes and leaving them to sort themselves out. This attitude is very much a reflection of what another American expert on quality improvement, Joseph Juran, said about the causes of problems in organizations. He stated that 85% of an organization's problems are due to systems and the processes within them, rather than to the workers involved in those processes. Processes need to be continuously changed and improved if an organization is to provide quality products and services – and who better to suggest improvements than the staff involved in the processes? The following example illustrates how one just simple suggestion for an improvement can save time and money.

Ismail is a forklift driver on a construction site. He has worked on several sites in the past where things were in a mess, with materials lying in disorganized piles, packaging strewn all over the place, and empty forklift pallets scattered about. He is pleased to note that on this site the manager has got everything much more sorted out, and there is a place in one corner of the site for waste packaging to be collected, flattened and stacked, and for empty pallets to be stacked, each day. The only trouble is that if you happen to be working some distance from this stacking area, you can waste an awful lot of time driving across the site to reach it. Ismail wonders why they don't set up a second area on the opposite side of the site. He's sure it will save him 30 minutes a day. Multiply that by the number of forklift drivers and the construction company will be saving several hours per week that would be better spent ensuring supplies get to the various work-teams when they need them.

Convinced that his idea is a good one, he suggests it to the site manager. Fortunately, the manager is committed to the idea of continuous improvement and decides to act on Ismail's suggestion.

What, would have happened if the manager wasn't committed to continuous improvement? The answer is possibly nothing at all – in which case, Ismail would probably never make a suggestion for change again. For continuous improvement to happen, management throughout an organization must be committed to achieving it and work at creating positive attitudes to change at all levels over a period of time. So all staff need to develop a proactive attitude to change. When it happens as part of an ongoing programme of improvement, they need to learn to welcome, rather than fear, it.

Activity 18 · 4 mins

Think about your own personal attitude to change. Do you fear it or welcome it? What are the reasons for your answer to this question?

_____

_____

_____

There are, of course, many reasons why people fear change. The most obvious one is that it will make their own situation worse rather than better. In some situations this is a perfectly justifiable reaction, as we will discuss in Session C. However, change can also be very positive.

3 The positive aspects of change

Change is an inevitable part of development, and it often brings hope and opportunity.

Activity 19

5 mins

How many positive aspects of change at work can you think of? For example, change can bring new interest to your job.

_____

_____

_____

_____

_____

_____

_____

Would you agree with the following?

- Change can bring **new interest** to the job.
  Almost all jobs can become tedious or uninteresting after a time. A change can have the effect of re-awakening enthusiasm and of stimulating a fresh appetite for the task.

- Change can open up new prospects for **career development**.
  Trying to make progress in your chosen career can sometimes feel the way the sailor feels, when trapped inshore in shallow water. No matter how much you desire to move on, there's nothing you can do about it – until the tide changes.

■ Change can show a **new slant on things**.
Doing the same job, in the same team, in the same way will make you start to believe there's no other way of doing it. It isn't until you break old habits that you see there are sides to the work you haven't thought of. Change will provoke discussion, raise new questions, give new food for thought.

■ Change can provide the opportunity to learn **new skills**.
New technology, new systems, new people – these may all bring with them the prospect of adding new strings to your bow.

■ Change can be a **challenge**.
Instituting change is a new adventure. You are a pioneer, an explorer of the unknown. Can you stay cool in the face of fire?

■ Change can provide an opportunity to **empower** the team: to give team members the scope and resources to gain more control over the work they do.

If you're concerned about motivation, the problem could be that your team members don't feel involved enough in their assigned tasks. When change occurs, it could be the right time to loosen the reins a little – or a lot.

To summarize, work is more rewarding for those who learn to identify the positive aspects of change.

Once you yourself are convinced of the positive aspects of change, you will be in a far better position to help create a culture in which everyone recognizes the benefits of change on a continuous basis.

4 Establishing a culture receptive to change

Managers cannot create an organizational quality culture in which people are ready to both initiate and adapt to change on their own – it has to be something that all managers, at all levels, throughout an organization are keen to be involved in. This doesn't mean that you shouldn't attempt to create a culture receptive to change within your own team, whatever the attitude of others in the organization. However, it will certainly be a lot easier for you to do this in some organizations than in others.

Activity 20 · ⏱ 5 mins

The table below consists of pairs of statements describing two very different types of organization. For each pair, give your organization a mark of between 1 and 5 according to where you think it lies on the scale between the two types. For example, if you think your organization is one in which all decisions are made at the top, give it a score of 1. If, however, you think it's an organization in which people at all levels have some responsibility for making decisions, give it a score of 5. Another possibility is that your organization may have handed down some responsibility for decisions, but – in your opinion – not enough, in which case you may give it a score of 3.

Organization A	Scale	Organization B
There is a high level of conflict within and between teams rather than mutual trust	1 2 3 4 5	Relations within, and between, teams are generally friendly and based on mutual trust
Managers work mostly behind closed doors and dislike being interrupted	1 2 3 4 5	Managers are generally considerate and supportive
All decisions are made at the top	1 2 3 4 5	Decisions are made at all levels
Everyone's job is precisely defined	1 2 3 4 5	People can change their work role in ways not defined in their job descriptions
All training follows a fixed pro-gramme	1 2 3 4 5	Training is given whenever the need for new skills is identified
All communications pass up and down through each level	1 2 3 4 5	Communications run across as well as up and down
Communications generally take the form of one-way commands	1 2 3 4 5	Communications are more like two-way consultations than one-way commands
People receive inadequate informa-tion about what is going on within the organization	1 2 3 4 5	People are kept well-informed about what is going on within the organization
Procedures are written in stone	1 2 3 4 5	Suggestions for improvements to pro-cedures are encouraged
People are expected to lead projects on the basis of orders from above	1 2 3 4 5	People are encouraged to guide pro-jects in the way they believe they will work

How did your organization score? If it scored between 40 and 50 points, you work in an organization where the staff are more ready to adapt to change and even initiate it themselves. If the score was at the lower end of the scale – under 15 points – your organization has a long way to go in creating a culture receptive to change.

As a first line manager, you can do little to change the culture of your organization on your own, but you can make some progress in developing in your own team, a culture that is receptive to change.

Activity 21 · 5 mins

Is the culture of your team one that encourages positive attitudes to change? If not, the way in which you run your team may be the reason. To find out tick the statements that best reflect your views. You can tick as many or as few as you want, but make sure you answer as honestly as possible.

I run my team based on the following beliefs.

a People only work hard when they have to – they need to be goaded into action. ☐

b People work hard when they feel they are working for their own benefit and what they do is meaningful to them. ☐

c It is important for the team that I am in control of everything that goes on. ☐

d It is best that all communications pass through formal channels; otherwise, there is chaos. ☐

e Everyone should be as fully informed as possible, because the most effective working relationships are based on a common understanding of needs. ☐

f Collaboration and informality work better than formality and withholding information. ☐

g Efficiency depends on everyone having a clearly defined job to do; that way everyone knows what is expected and the work is more easily controlled. ☐

h Efficiency depends on flexible arrangements, so that workteams can adapt to changing requirements more easily. People should be able to move freely from activity to activity, and work area to work area. ☐

i People work best at simple, undemanding tasks, so it is best to break down jobs into small parts and cut out the need for people lower down the organization to make decisions. ☐

j People work best if they are given complete and meaningful jobs to do. With the right opportunities for training, most people can cope with more difficult and demanding work, so it is best to keep variety and flexibility in jobs. ☐

According to the experience of most successful organizations, the philosophy expressed by (b), (e), (f), (h) and (j) above are more likely to encourage a positive attitude to change than the philosophy suggested by (a), (c), (d), (g) and (i).

As a first line manager, it is your responsibility to ensure that your team have the necessary information, knowledge and skills to adapt to, and initiate, change. You also need to help them feel that they 'own' any change they are involved in implementing. If they see change as something imposed upon 'us' by 'them', they will find it much more difficult to be enthusiastic about it.

Ownership is the key to success in implementing change. Those who feel they own something are much more likely to take care of it.

5 Promoting continuous improvement

You've seen that a readiness to initiate change is at the heart of any attempt to increase quality on a continuous basis. But how do you get people to take the first step in initiating change – and start making suggestions for improvements – if they have never done this before? Two frequently used methods are:

- suggestion schemes;
- quality circles.

5.1 Suggestion schemes

Suggestion schemes can be aimed at individuals or teams. Some companies, particularly Japanese companies, have made their suggestion schemes reward-based. Toyota, for example, treats all suggestions as valuable, and pays for them even if some result in the company making a loss. This is because it accepts that the top 2.5% of suggestions more than counter-balance the losses.

Your organization may not want to do the same, but if you receive suggestions, bear in mind two aspects of the Toyota approach. Whenever Toyota receives suggestions, they are:.

- acknowledged within 24 hours;
- evaluated within one week.

Activity 22 · 3 mins

Why do you think it is important to acknowledge ideas within 24 hours and evaluate them within one week?

_____

_____

_____

You probably know from your experience that it is very discouraging to come up with an idea, only to feel that it has disappeared into a black hole. If staff are to keep on making suggestions for improvements, they need to feel that their ideas are appreciated and taken seriously. If they have to wait too long for any considered response to their ideas, they are likely to lose interest.

5.2 Quality circles

A quality circle involves regular meetings of small group of volunteers who agree to:

- identify, analyse and propose solutions to problems;
- monitor the implementation of the planned solutions;
- present their findings to management.

To succeed, a quality circle must be supported by managers and its leaders must be given training in skills such as facilitating. In practice, a quality circle often makes a big impact initially as people voice all the ideas they've been having for months – perhaps years – and management listens carefully. Then, as more quality circles are established throughout the organization, managers find they cannot cope with going to all the meetings they are expected to attend. Without the support of management, people begin to lose interest and stop coming up with ideas.

As a first line manager, you can play a major role in facilitating a quality circle, though you will certainly need the ongoing support of your manager if the circle is to be successful.

Some ways of helping people to come up with ideas for improvements are:

- suggesting ideas yourself;
- using techniques like brainstorming to get ideas going;
- encouraging the group to 'build' people's ideas.

Brainstorming

Brainstorming is a skill that needs to be learned by both a group and its leader. It can be extremely effective if carried out well but have disappointing results if not conducted correctly.

In brainstorming you ask members of the group to give you whatever ideas come into their head relating to a particular problem or situation. As they voice their ideas:

- ■ you write exactly what they say on a flipchart;
- ■ you don't stop to discuss or evaluate any of the ideas.

Only when the brainstorm is complete do you start to discuss and evaluate ideas and draw up a shortlist of the ones that are most feasible.

Building ideas

So how do you decide which ideas are the most feasible? It isn't very helpful to go through the list and promptly discard those that, on the face of it, don't seem useful. A better course of action is to try and build the ideas before you judge them. Ask the following questions.

- ■ What's good about this idea?
- ■ How can it be improved?
- ■ Are there any ideas which might be combined with it?

Remember, the golden rule is not to judge or criticize an initial idea. Instead, focus on how it can be made to work.

Activity 23

Here is an example of how brainstorming and idea building can together lead to an improvement in a process.

Tamsin worked as Office Manager of a small company supplying stationery to businesses. The company offices were spread over three floors in which there was just one high-quality photocopying machine. Numerous problems were associated with this arrangement. For a start, the machine was not easy to use and some people always struggled to work out which buttons to press and exactly which way round to put their paper. The same people also had difficulties with reloading the machine with paper and didn't know what to do when the light came on indicating that the toner was running low. Furthermore, the machine frequently broke down. Then, when it was working there was often a queue of people wanting to use it. It was particularly annoying to go to the machine to make a single copy, only to find that someone was in the middle of doing a bulk job.

All this caused a lot of unnecessary annoyance and conflict, so Tamsin decided it was time she and her team looked into the photocopying situation. At a meeting she wrote up the full list of problems and then led the team in a brainstorm for ideas on how to solve them. Among the ideas they came up with were:

- get rid of the big photocopier;
- put a small photocopier on every floor;
- appoint someone to make sure the photocopier is loaded with paper at the beginning of the day;
- put someone in charge of making sure that the toner is not about to run out;
- send bulk photocopying to a photocopier shop;
- appoint people to deal with problems like jammed paper;
- organize training for all staff on how to use the machine.

None of these ideas would provide the whole solution on their own, but combined and developed they could provide the company with the photocopying service it needs.

If you were Tamsin, how would you suggest combining and developing the various ideas that came out of the brainstorming session?

_____
_____
_____
_____
_____
_____
_____
_____
_____
_____

Getting rid of the present big photocopier seems like a good idea – it breaks down far too often. However, a photocopier with the full range of facilities for enlarging, reducing, doing double-sided copies, and so on might be very necessary for the business. Perhaps the next step is to do some research on alternative photocopiers and their maintenance agreements. It is also a good idea to put a small photocopier on every floor. This will reduce the time people waste walking between floors to the photocopier and standing in queues. A possible next step is to decide how many copies people should be able to do on the small photocopiers, and in what situations they should use the large photocopier. Appointing someone, possibly on each floor, to take responsibility for filling up the copier with paper each morning, keeping an eye on the toner, and generally being on call to deal with problems might be a good idea. But this could become an onerous duty. It might be better to give a number of staff some proper training in how to operate the copiers and draw up a monthly rota for taking responsibility for the machine on your floor. Finally, whether it's a good idea to send bulk photocopying to a photocopier shop depends partly on whether this makes sense financially. Someone needs to conduct a cost-benefit analysis that takes into account how much staff time will be saved for other tasks by not having to do bulk photocopying in the office. (You can find what's involved in doing a cost-benefit analysis in the workbook in this series entitled *Making a Financial Case*.)

5.3 Communication

We have already seen that it is pointless to set up suggestions schemes and quality circles unless all levels of management are committed to creating a quality culture with a focus on continuous improvement. If this management commitment exists, one of the essentials for creating and maintaining commitment among staff is good communication. Your team will need to know:

■ what the quality programme and continuous improvement entail;
■ the targets or standards they should aim to meet;
■ their roles and responsibilities;
■ the training and support they will receive.

Activity 24 · 4 mins

What methods might be used to communicate everything staff need to know about a quality programme and maintain their commitment:

■ by your organization?
■ by you within your team?

_____

_____

_____

The organization as a whole might use circulars, regular emails, posters, newsletters, meetings, seminars and study days. Within your team you need to hold formal regular meetings to keep people informed and discuss possible improvements in processes, products and services. You also need to make sure you have frequent one-to-one conversations with individual members. These conversations should provide an opportunity for staff to express their views and experiences about changes initiated through a programme of continuous improvement.

In this session we have focused on what's involved in getting people committed to the idea of continuous improvement. How to build on this commitment, to ensure that processes, products and services really are improved on a continuous basis, is the subject of another book in this series entitled *Managing Change*.

Self-assessment 2 · 20 mins

1 Complete the diagram of the continuous improvement cycle by filling in the three missing words.

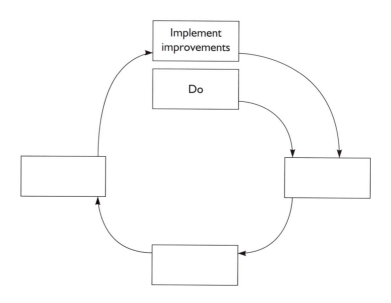

2 Complete the following sentences.

Providing quality products or services means meeting the _____ of customers at _____ they can afford. In today's competitive world, organizations should aim to actually exceed the _____ of their customers. They can only do this through continuous improvement of their products and services, which in turn means continuous improvement of their _____ . Continuous improvement results in constant _____ .

3   Which of the following statements do you agree with and which do you disagree with? Briefly explain your answer in each case.

   a   Change can add interest to a job.

      Agree/Disagree _____

      _____

   b   Change may give you some new ideas but it will never give you the opportunity to learn new skills.

      Agree/Disagree _____

      _____

   c   Change can provide an opportunity to give team members more control over what they do.

      Agree/Disagree _____

      _____

4   The following are statements about a culture receptive to change. Which are true and which are false?

   a   All decisions are made at the top.   TRUE/FALSE
   b   Suggestions for improvements to procedures are encouraged. TRUE/FALSE
   c   There is a high level of conflict within and between teams.   TRUE/FALSE
   d   Managers are generally considerate and supportive.   TRUE/FALSE

5   If a suggestion scheme is to be successful, there are two things you should aim to do in response to each suggestion. The first is to acknowledge it within 24 hours. What is the other?

   _____

6   Which of the following forms of communication do you NOT need in order to maintain commitment among staff to continuous improvement?

   a   Written information from managers to staff.
   b   Regular meetings between managers and staff as a group.
   c   Appraisal meetings with individual members of staff.
   d   Informal one-to-one conversations between managers and staff.

Answers to these questions can be found on page 79.

6 Summary

- Providing quality products and services means meeting customer needs at prices they can afford.

- The continuous improvement of processes is essential to increasing the quality of products and services.

- The continuous improvement cycle consists of :

  - doing;
  - reviewing what has been done;
  - learning from this review;
  - planning on the basis of what you have learnt;
  - doing what you have planned;
  - reviewing and learning from this, and so on.

- Continuous improvement means constant change.

- Change has many positive elements. It can:

  - bring new interest to a job;
  - open up new prospects for career development;
  - show a new slant on things;
  - provide the opportunity to learn new skills;
  - be a challenge;
  - provide an opportunity to empower the team.

- The culture of an organization can play a major part in encouraging people to both initiate and adapt to change.

- The ideal culture for change is one in which relations between and within teams are generally friendly and based on mutual trust, managers are supportive, information is shared, and people at all levels can make decisions.

- Two ways of encouraging people to come up with ideas for improvements are:

  - suggestion schemes;
  - quality circles.

- The techniques of brainstorming and building ideas are useful for encouraging people to come up with ideas for improvements within quality circles.

- Both formal and informal communication are essential for creating and maintaining of commitment to continuous improvement among staff.

Session C
Identifying and overcoming barriers to change

1 Introduction

Have you ever had the experience of being summoned into your manager's office to be told that there are going to be some changes – perhaps in the way the company is structured, or in the IT systems it uses, or even in the location of its offices? If so, what was your reaction? Did your heart sink at the prospect of more change and the upheaval involved? You wouldn't be unusual if you thought 'Oh no!' We all know that we live in a changing world, but this doesn't necessarily make it easier to cope with change when it comes – particularly when it's imposed by others.

So far we have focused on the role that you and your staff can play in initiating change. But change at work is often imposed on us by other parts of the organization or by senior management. Your opinions and ideas may be taken into account in the planning process, but your freedom to choose what course of action to take will probably be limited.

EXTENSION 1
For a classic account of the ability of organizations to change, and how people respond to change, try reading extension 1, *The Change Masters* by Rosabeth Moss Kanter.

In such situations you may feel resistance to change – and you will almost certainly encounter it in others. So how do you overcome this resistance, both within yourself and in others, and get people to focus on the positive aspects of change wherever they exist?

2 Resistance to change in yourself

Before you can begin to overcome your own resistance to change, you need to think about the reasons for the resistance.

Activity 25 · · · · · 4 mins

Put yourself in the position of a manager whose team or department is being 'investigated' with a view to changing it. Why might you react in a negative way? What reasons might you have to fear change?

Spend a few minutes thinking about this and then write down your response briefly.

_____

_____

_____

_____

If you are like most people, you might well resent the interference of the investigation. But your reaction to what you see as the threat of change could be:

■ fear that you will lose your status or position;
■ worry that your career prospects will suffer;
■ anxiety about consequent loss of earnings.

You may see change as a threat to position, prospects or prosperity. In addition, you may feel:

■ anger that all the work you have done to build up the present system may now be thrown away;
■ that you aren't in control of your own destiny;
■ general uncertainty.

Resistance to change is a natural reaction, but, as we discussed in Session B, most changes bring benefits as well as problems. Furthermore, as a manager you should be ready to take the lead in overcoming your initial negative reactions and focus on how to respond in a constructive way to suggestions for change.

Activity 26

3 mins

Suppose you are told, as a first line manager, that there is to be a new paperwork system covering your team's work. The only thing you've heard about the new system is that it seems complicated, although you assume that it does have some advantages. How would you react, do you think?

_____

_____

_____

_____

_____

You might react by:

■ questioning why a new system is needed, because the old one seems perfectly adequate;

■ groaning inwardly, knowing how hard it is to get people to use a new system;

■ reserving judgement, until you've learned how the new system works and what advantages it offers;

■ wondering why these bureaucrats have time to invent paperwork systems when you're so busy.

The chances are that you will have mixed reactions, but you may decide to respond by being diplomatic and giving your full co-operation. You know that, as a first line manager, you are expected to make things work, even if you have misgivings about what is being suggested.

Activity 27 · 4 mins

As a team leader, with the normal tendency to tend to resist change, but also an intelligent responsible member of the organization, how do you think you should react to proposals for change? Write down two positive, responsible ways to respond.

_____

_____

_____

_____

_____

_____

There's no point in being negative, is there? After all, if you greet the proposals with scepticism and resentment, what can you expect from your workteam? The only sensible approach is to be open minded and positive. You could have suggested the following.

■ Forgetting vested interests.
   You may feel that the time and energy you've spent on the old system will now be wasted, but this shouldn't prevent you looking seriously at the new scheme.

■ Setting aside your prejudices.
   We all have our opinions and preferences, but know that we ought not to let them cloud our judgement. (Nevertheless, if you have ideas of your own – perhaps you can see a better way of doing things – you might reasonably request an opportunity to present them.)

■ Learning more about the new system.
   Any new scheme must have its merits; the more you understand it, the easier it will be to work with it.

■ Using your knowledge to help the workteam.
   Because you recognize your own resistance to change, you can help overcome it in others.

3 Acknowledging resistance to change in others

<table>
<tr><td>Apprehension and doubt about proposed changes are to be expected.</td><td>When faced with the prospect of change, people will often react by seeing it as a threat, especially when the implications of the change haven't been discussed with them, for example when a company announces a major change of policy and approach.</td></tr>
</table>

Activity 28 · 6 mins

Imagine that your organization has announced a new 'customer awareness' programme, in the face of a growing number of customer complaints. The directors have made it clear that everyone will have to become more proactive in customer care. A series of seminars on the subject are to be held, which everyone will be expected to attend.

Your team normally has minimum contact with customers. Before the programme starts you talk to them about it to get their reactions. What sort of thing might they say? Write down two or three sentences of imagined conversations.

_____

_____

_____

_____

_____

_____

Here are some typical reactions.

- 'I hope this is not just another management gimmick.'
- 'This has nothing to do with us. We never see the customer.'

- 'I'm not a sales or marketing person. I'm not even very good at talking to people. How will I cope?'
- 'Will this mean that we all have to start wearing smart suits?'
- 'Will we now be judged on how well we can chat people up? I'm a specialist, not a salesperson.'
- 'Just when I'd got this job taped up, they want to change everything. Why can't things go on as they did before? I thought it was all going well.'

There is invariably an initial resistance to change. It's the kind of situation where, as a first line manager, you will need all your skills of tact and persuasion. In fact, you will need to think very carefully about how to introduce a programme for change to your team – something that the manager featured in the next Activity clearly failed to do.

Activity 29

3 mins

The workteam knew that their team leader, Piers Loman, had been attending an important meeting with senior management. When he came back to the shop floor, several of his team looked at him expectantly.

'I can't say anything except that there will be a lot of changes around here,' Piers said. 'You'll probably be told more next week.'

How do you think the team would react to a statement like that?

_____

_____

_____

It wouldn't be surprising if the team members stopped work, as soon as the leader's back was turned, to speculate about the possible changes. How could they be expected to concentrate with something like that hanging over their heads?

Unspecified changes will evoke strong emotions: often a mixture of anxiety, excitement and hope. Change is threatening – and at the same time offers new possibilities for the future.

Let's continue the story.

Activity 30

3 mins

The following week Piers gathered the workteam together and made an announcement.

'I can now reveal to you that the job we are currently doing will cease as from this Friday. But there's no need for any of you to be concerned. You will all be re-assigned to new duties. Of course, it will mean that many of you will have to be given training in new skills. Jean Winkler and I will be discussing your new jobs with you as soon as possible. Meanwhile, just relax and don't worry.'

Do you imagine that the team members with take Piers' last piece of advice? How do you think they will react now?

_____

_____

_____

_____

_____

If they had difficulty concentrating on their work after Piers' earlier remarks, the team members are now likely to have trouble sleeping at night as well! What the manager has just said is that the whole of their working lives will change – and he expects them to relax!

Not giving out information about a forthcoming change, or handing it out piecemeal, leads to great uncertainty in people. And this uncertainty is one of the main reasons·for them feeling negative about the prospect of change.

Let's be honest: this kind of situation is not exactly unknown, is it? In many companies, drastic changes are planned without consulting the people most affected by them. And information is handed out piecemeal, so provoking the kind of negative reactions they would prefer to avoid.

Activity 31 ·

We've already discussed the fact that people need information. Piers Loman is apparently giving his team all the information he has, so where is he going wrong? What should he have done differently? Think this over for a few minutes and then write down your ideas.

_____

_____

_____

_____

_____

In fact, Piers has not really given very much in the way of useful information. He has let it be known that drastic changes are planned, which will affect the working lives of his team members. Without any information on just how each person will be affected, this is worse than knowing nothing.

It would have been better if Piers had said nothing – and preferably not have even disclosed at the start the fact that he was going to an important meeting.

Only when he had sat down with this manager (or whoever else was involved) and worked out what the main implications would be, should he have made any announcement. This is not withholding information – it is preparing information so that it can be used effectively.

Of course, he might have to act quickly.

Activity 32 ·

3 mins

Why might Piers have to work hard to get the details out quickly? What is the danger here?

_____

_____

_____

_____

The danger is that the rumours of impending change may get out before all the details can be prepared. In many places of work there is a 'grapevine' which is capable of spreading information and misinformation very quickly. Piers would be under great pressure if news of the proposals are 'leaked', because the rumours would tend to have a similar effect to a premature announcement.

These kinds of decisions are never easy: when to make announcements of change, what to say, who to tell first. They are not easy for any level of management. The important thing to bear in mind is that disturbing news is bound to upset people, so:

it is important to think through the consequences of announcements about change

4 Managing resistance to change

We have seen that resistance to change is normal, and that its underlying causes are:

- a perceived threat to position, prosperity or prospects;
- the natural inclination to hang on to what you know, rather than embrace something that is unfamiliar;
- uncertainty.

Normal as it is, this doesn't change the fact that you will often have to overcome resistance to change. So how do you go about doing this?

One of the first things you can do is to think carefully about the precise nature of the forces opposed to the change – and then identify those forces that are behind the change. Identifying these forces is what is known as a 'force field analysis'.

4.1 Force field analysis

You may remember that in Activity 28 we considered the reactions of staff to the announcement of a new customer awareness programme. All took the form of objections, each of which could be seen as a force opposing change – for example:

- the suspicion that this was just another management gimmick that would not amount to much in reality;
- the feeling that the new programme had nothing to do with them as they rarely saw a customer;
- the belief that they did not have sufficient marketing and selling skills to be able to contribute to the programme effectively;
- a general fear of the unknown.

In the Activity we didn't consider the positive reactions people might have had, each of which could be seen as a force supporting change. They might have included:

- the feeling among some staff that their jobs might become more interesting;
- appreciation of the opportunity to acquire new knowledge and skills;
- relief that something is going to be done about the increasing number of customer complaints.

Of course, the forces that will support or oppose a change do not only reflect the attitudes of staff. There are other forces that come from both within and outside the organization. In our example, the supporting forces include the growing number of customer complaints and the decision of management to introduce a new customer care programme. The opposing forces include the disruption caused by staff attending a series of seminars.

Once you have considered what the 'supporting' and 'opposing' forces are, the next step is to map out these forces in a diagram, such as the one below. Begin by drawing a horizontal line. Next, list the supporting forces above the line and the opposing forces below the line. If possible, draw arrows of varying thickness to indicate the comparative strength of each force.

Supporting Forces

Determination of directors to introduce programme	Growing number of customer complaints	Relief that action to be taken	Appreciation of opportunity to learn new skills	Belief among staff that job interest will increase

Suspicion that it is a management gimmick	Disruption caused by seminars	Feeling among some staff that programme is nothing to do with them	Belief among staff that they lack necessary skills	General fear of the unknown

Opposing Forces

Once you have produced this diagram you can start thinking about ways of:

- maintaining the supporting forces at their present level;
- reducing the opposing forces.

What you definitely shouldn't do is ignore the opposing forces and just concentrate on further strengthening the supporting forces. If you do, you will probably end up increasing resistance! Returning to our example, if management were to react to grumbles among the staff by simply repeating their determination to introduce the customer awareness programme, this would only increase the grumbles.

Activity 33

5 mins

If you were the manager of a team who had just been told about a new customer awareness programme, what would you do to reduce the opposing forces?

_____

_____

_____

_____

You might stress that management were actually concerned about the level of customer complaints and were serious about improving customer care. You might point out that customer care is a lot more than speaking politely to customers: that it's fundamentally about ensuring that customer needs are met through improving the quality of products or services while continuing to provide them at a price the customers can afford. This means that you don't have to have everyday contact with customers in order to contribute to customer care. You might also emphasize that staff will be equipped with any necessary new skills through training and that the programme represents an opportunity for all staff to expand their jobs and make them more interesting. There are many positive elements in change, including the fact that it brings new challenges and new interest to a job.

Activity 34 · 10 mins

S/NVQ C12.1

This Activity may provide the basis of appropriate evidence for your S/NVQ portfolio. If you are intending to take this course of action, it might be better to write your answer on separate sheets of paper.

Think about a significant change in which and your team you have recently been involved.

What would you say were the forces supporting change?

_____

_____

_____

_____

What were the forces opposing change?

_____

_____

_____

_____

What, if anything, did you do to maintain the supporting forces and decrease the opposing forces?

_____

_____

_____

_____

Thinking about the change again, what more might you have done in response to the opposing forces?

_____

_____

_____

_____

4.2 Unfreezing, movement and refreezing

The stage during which you identify and work on the forces for and against change, and so create a climate in which change can more easily take place, is often called 'unfreezing'. Put another way, unfreezing 'warms people up' to the idea of change. During this stage it is essential to have two-way communication, in which you discuss with people:

- why the proposed change is necessary – that is, what problems the change is intended to solve;
- the benefits of the change;
- what new skills the change will give staff the opportunity to acquire.

You also need to give people the opportunity to talk about their worries and provide them with reassurance.

Once people have got used to the idea of change, you are ready to progress to the movement stage, when change actually begins to happen. The key to success in this stage is ensuring that people have a sense of ownership. This means giving them the opportunity to **participate** in the planning of how the change is to be implemented. It also means giving them the **information**, knowledge and skills they need to handle the change. Finally, to implement change successfully you need to demonstrate **enthusiasm**.

You can remember the three main ingredients of the recipe for successful change implementation by the letters PIE.

- Participation
- Information
- Enthusiasm

Once the change has taken place we come to the refreezing stage, when people settle down into the new way of doing things. We'll return to the stage of refreezing at the end of this session, but first we're going to look in more detail at PIE.

4.3 Participation

Activity 35

5 mins

Suppose your team has been assigned some new equipment to help you do your job more efficiently. The equipment is due to arrive in a month's time. Your main concern is that the team members will have to change their ways of working, learn how to use the equipment, but continue to be a productive unit during the period of change-over.

You decide that your first priority is to get every team member thinking in a positive way about the change,

How would you approach this task? Jot down your thoughts briefly.

_____

_____

_____

_____

One approach is to describe the equipment to the team and point out that it is designed to make the job easier. This would certainly help to overcome any scepticism – people are obviously much happier to accept a change if they see it as helping to lessen their workload.

However, the worth of the equipment has yet to be proven, so it may be seen as just another problem. A way to overcome this is to invite the team to participate in planning for the change. If people are involved in solving a mutual problem, they tend to concentrate on helping each other, rather than worrying about the effects on them personally.

How you go about this will depend on you and your team. You might feel it best to start by holding a general discussion, with you standing at a blackboard or flip-chart, writing down the points as they arise. The starting point could be: 'This is the new equipment. It looks like it could be useful to us. What we have to decide is how to get the most from it without letting it disrupt our normal work. I need your ideas. In fact, I will need you to organize the whole business.'

Or you might involve more senior members of the team first, perhaps putting the problem as 'How do we get these youngsters to cope with the new equipment?'

You know your team best, and what they are capable of, so there is no single approach that will work in all circumstances. One thing is certain, however:

where change is concerned, participation is the best antidote to resistance.

4.4 Information

As has been suggested before, one of the main causes of negative and emotional reactions to change is uncertainty.

The best cure for the anguish of uncertainty is information.

Projected change provokes questions. If the questions go unanswered, they become problems; and the problems, real or imagined, will undermine the effectiveness of the plans.

Activity 36 · 5 mins

Suppose you are in charge of the day-to-day running of a branch of a building society. The management have found new premises in the town and you are made responsible for planning and organizing the move. You are determined to keep the team fully informed, so as to avoid problems arising from uncertainty.

What actions could you take to do this effectively? Think about this for a few minutes, then write down at least three things that you might do.

_____

_____

_____

_____

_____

Some ways of keeping the team informed during a move, would be to:

■ show them the new premises, collectively and/or individually: where they will work, the facilities available and so on;

■ hold a meeting in which you announce details of the move, followed by a discussion session in which you do your best to answer any questions that arise;

■ extend an invitation to all members of the team to discuss privately any particular problems they foresee, so you can try to overcome them together and allay any fears;

■ make it clear to each person what part they have to play during the changeover, including what they should tell their customers and so on.

Information is the best medicine for uncertainty.

4.5 Enthusiasm

It almost goes without saying that the team leader has to try to inspire enthusiasm, because enthusiasm helps smooth out the snags.

If the team members see that their leader is lukewarm and half-hearted about the proposals for change, they will tend to act in the same way.

Leaders of change who show fire and fervour are likely to carry the team along with them.

Enthusiasm is infectious.

Of course, in reality it is sometimes hard to be enthusiastic. What do you do if you have serious misgivings about a proposed change, or the way you've been told it is to be implemented?

Activity 37 · 5 mins

Imagine your company announces a new bonus scheme to replace an earlier one. You, along with other first line managers, are told about this and instructed to pass on details to your team. Initially, you sit down and work out that your team will be worse off than before, whereas most other teams will benefit from the new scheme.

What can you do? How can you go along to your team and enthusiastically announce the scheme knowing that your group will be out of pocket? Think about how you would handle a situation like this.

Which of the following would you do?

- Pretend to your team that there really is no difference between the two schemes?
- Blame it all on management and say that it isn't your fault?
- Ask for an urgent discussion with your manager to point out the problem and ask for some changes to the scheme?
- Go to your manager and say that it's up to him or her to tell the team, as you don't want to be the unpopular one?
- Take some other action (write down your ideas here)?

_____

_____

_____

_____

Your options may be limited but you at least have to explore them all. What you **can't** do is go along to the team and say: 'Management have really done it to us this time!' because team morale will sink to rock bottom and create a rift in the company that may be hard to repair. Team leaders have to represent the workteam appropriately to management, and management properly to the team, or nothing they try to achieve will work well.

Also, there's no point in pretending that there isn't a problem. People are very quick to realize that their income has been reduced, and then you would either look foolish or dishonest – or both.

Your best option in this case may be to request an urgent discussion of the matter with your manager, in which you point out the negative effects of the change, and perhaps ask whether your team can be compensated for their losses in some way. You might even propose an alternative scheme or a modification to the proposals. After all, the idea of bonus schemes is to provide an incentive to work harder. It isn't in the company's interests for them to have the opposite effect.

There are other kinds of situations where you may not agree with the changes proposed, yet accept the fact that they are inevitable. A company that is losing money may have to make some personnel redundant, for instance, or even close a part of its operation. These changes are always hard to face, and enthusiasm doesn't come into it. The best you can do is try to soften the blow as much as circumstances allow.

EXTENSION 2
A useful guide to leading teams through the process of change is provided by extension 2, *Handbook for Creative Team Leaders* by Tudor Rickards and Susan Moger.

Once you have explored every aspect of the change proposals with which you disagree, and have done all you can to put forward your own and your team's point of view, then all that is left is:

to be as positive and open-minded as you can.

4.6 The refreezing stage

The term 'refreezing' might imply to you that once you have gone through a period of change, everything settles down again into a new stable situation. In fact, this isn't quite true. As change is a constant feature of life, no one can expect that once a change has taken place there won't be another. However, the refreezing stage acknowledges that it always takes time for people to become accustomed to using new skills and knowledge and practising new ways of working. You can't necessarily expect the same level of efficiency and performance straight away.

Activity 38

4 mins

As a first line manager, you need to be alert to any problems arising from the implementation of change, and take whatever steps you can to minimize them. Which of the following courses of action do you think would be most suitable during the refreezing stage? Tick more than one box if you wish.

a Being receptive to feedback, as you want to get the team involved. ☐

b Not taking too much notice of comments, on the grounds that all changes are bound to bring a few grumbles. ☐

c Insisting that everything is done as was originally planned. ☐

d Being prepared to make adjustments to the original plan for change in the light of experience and new knowledge. ☐

e Seeking the opinions of the workteam on the effects of the change. ☐

(a), (d) and (e) are probably the most appropriate and effective way to behave. Plans are seldom put into effect without modification, because it is very difficult for planners to foresee all the consequences of the change. During

EXTENSION 3
You will find an overview of the many aspects of organizational change in extension 3, *Managing Change* by Robert Heller.

the refreezing stage, snags and problems will inevitably arise. As a leader of change, you need to watch out for these, listen to the comments of team members and be prepared to make adjustments.

Being a leader of change requires the ability to be flexible.

Self-assessment 3 ·

10 mins

1   In each of the following statements, pick the one word or phrase that is the most suitable.

a Resistance to change is INAPPROPRIATE/DESIRABLE/NORMAL.
b People often resist change because of GENERAL UNCERTAINTY/ CERTAINTY THAT IT WILL MAKE THINGS WORSE.
c As a manager you should focus on how to respond to proposals for change in a QUESTIONING/DIPLOMATIC/CONSTRUCTIVE way.

2   The missing word in the following statement begins with P. What is it?

Among the main underlying causes of people's resistance to change is that they see it as a threat to their position, prospects and _____.

3   In any change situation, there will be forces supporting and forces opposing the change. When faced with forces opposed to change, which **two** of the following should you do?

- Increase the supporting forces.
- Maintain the supporting forces at their present level.
- Reduce the opposing forces.
- Ignore the opposing forces.

4   Fill in the missing words.

a Where change is concerned, _____ is the best antidote to resistance.

b _____ is the best medicine for uncertainty.

c _____ is infectious.

INFORMATION   PLANNING   ENTHUSIASM

CHANGE   PARTICIPATION   ASSERTIVENESS

Answers to these questions can be found on page 80.

5 Summary

- Resistance to change is normal.

- When you react negatively to the prospect of change, it may be because you see it as a threat to position, prospects or prosperity, or because you are uncertain about what it will bring.

- As a manager, you need to take the lead in overcoming your initial negative reactions to proposals for change and focus on how to respond in a constructive way.

- Before announcing any major change, it is essential to know what the main implications of that change will be.

- In any change situation, there will be forces supporting and forces opposing the change. As a leader of change, you need to work on maintaining the forces that support a change and reducing those that oppose it.

- Two-way communication has a major role to play in preparing people for change during the 'unfreezing stage' of a change programme.

- The three main ingredients of the recipe for successful change implementation are as follows.
  - Participation
  - Information
  - Enthusiasm

- Where change is concerned, participation is the best antidote to resistance.

- Information is the best medicine for uncertainty arising from change.

- In reality, it is sometimes hard to be enthusiastic. In situations where you do not agree with the proposed changes that you have been asked to implement, you may have to settle for being as positive and open-minded as you can.

- During the 'refreezing' stage, you need to:
  - be receptive to feedback from the team;
  - be prepared to make adjustments to the original plan;
  - seek the opinions of your team on the effects of the change.

Performance checks

1 Quick quiz

Jot down the answers to the following questions on *Understanding Change*.

Question 1   What are the six kinds of forces for change represented by the initials PESTLE?

_____

_____

Question 2   Give two examples of how environmental forces for change that have affected organizations in the last 30 years or so.

_____

_____

_____

Question 3   What do the initials SWOT stand for?

_____

_____

Question 4   In the cycle of continuous improvement, you do something and then review what has been done. What are the next two steps?

_____

_____

_____

Question 5   List three positive aspects of change.

_____

_____

_____

Question 6   Name two features of a culture that is receptive to change.

_____

_____

_____

Question 7   Name two methods for encouraging people to start coming up with ideas for change as part of a continuous improvement programme.

_____

_____

Question 8   There are various techniques you can use in a meeting to get people to come up with ideas for improvements. Name two of them.

_____

_____

Question 9   If you were asked to summarize the 'normal' or typical reaction to an unexpected job change, what would you say?

_____

_____

Question 10   Name two of the methods that can be used by an organization to communicate everything staff need to know about a quality programme.

_____

_____

Question 11   Briefly, how would you instil a feeling of ownership for planned change in a workteam?

_____

_____

_____

Question 12   What do you identify when you carry out a force field analysis?

_____

_____

Question 13   What do the letters PIE stand for in the 'recipe' for overcoming resistance to change?

_____

Question 14   What is meant by 'unfreezing' and 'refreezing' in connection with change?

_____

_____

_____

Question 15   As a team leader, what are two of the suitable courses of action for you in the refreezing stage?

_____

_____

_____

Answers to these questions can be found on page 80.

2 Workbook assessment

60 mins

Imagine you work for a small organization (with anything between 20 and 50 employees) and you have been asked by your manager to attend a meeting at which ideas are to be discussed on how to attract – and keep – more customers for the organization's product of service. Your manager wants you think about what is happening outside the organization as well as within in.

■   How will you go about preparing for this meeting?

Write a paragraph on what you will do.

Some weeks after this meeting, your manager tells you that the organization has decided to make a number of important changes, one of which will mean some restructuring. There will be no redundancies, but people will be moved into different departments and will have to acquire some new skills. You will end up with a department consisting of two of your present staff and two new staff.

Consider the following questions.

■ What difficulties are there likely to be?
■ How you will go about preparing your staff for the change?
■ How you will help your staff through the actual change?
■ How will you try to deal with any worries or problems among your staff after the change?

Write a paragraph on each of these questions.

Make any assumptions you wish about the kind of work that the company does. If you wish, you can base any details not defined above on your own job, or one that you have done in the past.

Your complete answer to this assessment need not be longer than a single page.

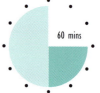

3 Work-based assignment

60 mins

S/NVQ A1.3

The time for this assignment gives you an approximate idea of how long it is likely to take you to write up your findings. You will find you need to spend some additional time gathering information, perhaps talking to colleagues and thinking about the assignment.

This assignment may provide the basis of appropriate evidence for your S/NVQ portfolio. The assignment is designed to help you demonstrate the following personal competences

■ building teams;
■ communicating;
■ focusing on results;
■ thinking and taking decisions.

What you have to do

For this assignment you are asked to identify and plan how to implement a significant change for your team that will bring about improvements in the way that they work. Start by using the outcomes of Activities 6, 8, 11, 12, 14, 15 and 34 to help you identify what changes are needed and why.

You should involve your team in agreeing the pressures for change and what changes are needed. You should also consult others who may be affected, especially your manager, and collect whatever data is needed to help you understand the factors that will influence its success or failure.

You should then interview three people likely to be affected by the change and ask them these questions.

- How will they be affected by it?
- What is their initial response to the change?
- How do they think they and the team will manage to adapt to the change?

You should record your findings, and then try to decide what can be deduced from the information you have gleaned. Your overall aim in this assignment is to answer the following questions.

- How will people react to the change?
- What resistance to change is likely to occur and what can be done to overcome it?
- What is likely to be the best strategy to lead people through the three stages of the process of change: unfreezing, movement and refreezing?
- What is my role going to be in making the change happen?
- How will the organizational culture help or hinder the change?
- How will you ensure everyone who needs to be is kept informed about the process of change?

What you have to write

Write down your recommendations and your plan for bringing about the change as a proposal to your manager or other relevant person. The whole document does not have to be more than two or three pages long. Include this written recommendation plus any supporting evidence in your portfolio.

Reflect and review

1 Reflect and review

Now that you have completed your work on *Understanding Change*, let's review our workbook objectives together.

The first workbook objective was as follows.

■ You should be better able to identify the forces behind change and how they might affect your organization and team.

We reviewed six major forces behind changes of all kinds: political, economic, social, technological, legal and environmental factors. Political factors arise from the policies pursued by the government of the day, some of which may have an effect on economic factors. In fact, it's not always easy to decide whether a factor is political or economic. Of course, some economic factors have nothing to do with government policies, arising as they do out of events beyond the government's control.

Social factors may be long term – such as changes in the composition of the population – or fleeting, as in the case of fashion in clothes and food. The same can be said of technology, which drives change along at a relentless pace. New laws and regulations, some of them relating to environmental issues such as pollution and the need to preserve finite resources, also bring about change, as do environmental developments themselves and the public's response to them.

As a leader of change, it is useful for you to be able to identify which of these factors are in operation when a change occurs at work. It is even more valuable to make yourself aware of known developments so that you can identify possible threats or opportunities for your organization. Such threats and opportunities could lead to changes with possible effects on both you and your team.

You may want to ask yourself the following questions regarding these points.

- To what extent do I spend time considering the causes of change in my work?

  _____

  _____

  _____

- How could I find out more about events which may result in changes in my organization, and so possibly in my job and the jobs of my team, in the future?

  _____

  _____

  _____

The second workbook objective was as follows.

- You should be better able to recognize the beneficial aspects of change, whether it be through continuous improvement or through one-off projects.

We have looked at both the 'up' and the 'down' sides of change. When change takes place as part of a programme of continuous improvement aimed at increasing quality, it can be initiated by any member of a team. It does not necessarily provoke the negative feelings people often have in response to change imposed by senior management. These negative feelings, along with any drawbacks of a proposed change, need to be recognized from the outset if they are not to present unexpected snags.

However, you and your team will stand to benefit most from a change if you are able to recognize and communicate its good points. These include:

- bringing **new interest** to the job;
- opening up new prospects for **career development**;
- showing a **new slant on things**;
- providing the opportunity to learn **new skills**;
- posing a **challenge**;
- giving an opportunity to **empower** the team.

You may feel the following questions are appropriate when considering the implications of a proposal.

■ How can I and my team members get the most from this change?

_____

_____

_____

■ In what ways can the change be used as a step towards new career developments for each of us?

_____

_____

_____

■ How can we meet the challenge of this change and find new interest in the work through it?

_____

_____

_____

■ What is good about this change?

_____

_____

_____

The next workbook objective was as follows.

■ You should be better able to take a proactive role, and encourage others to take a proactive role, in initiating change.

Being aware of the forces for change and the threats and opportunities they pose to your organization will give you ideas on what changes your organization might make. And being aware of your organization's strengths and weaknesses will help you to decide which of your ideas could, or should, be acted on. However, as a first line manager you are far more likely to be able to initiate change as part of a programme of continuous improvement. In such a programme all staff are encouraged to make suggestions for improvement, and you have an important role to play not only in making suggestions yourself but in encouraging others to do so.

You may want to consider the following two questions in relation to these points.

■ Do I spend enough time each week thinking about possible improvements to the way things are done? If not, how can I ensure that I do so in the future?

_____

_____

_____

■ How can I encourage my team to make suggestions for improvements in the way things are done?

_____

_____

_____

Our final objective was as follows.

■ You should be better able to anticipate and recognize reactions to a proposed change, and overcome resistance to the change.

Reactions, as we have seen, will depend very much on:

■ the way that a change is presented;
■ how well the team leader or manager is able to 'sell' the idea of the change;
■ how much thought is given to the way in which information is released.

No matter how you present a change, you have to be prepared for at least some resistance to it. In the initial stages of a change project you need to consider the exact nature of this resistance and what you can do to reduce it – two-way communication will play a key role here. Once the change is underway, you can smooth its progress by ensuring that:

■ the team has the opportunity to participate in the planning process;
■ team members are given the information, knowledge and skills they need to handle the change;
■ you demonstrate enthusiasm – bearing in mind that in some situations this just isn't possible.

You might like to ask the following questions.

■ What can I do to improve my ability to recognize and anticipate reactions among my team?

_____

_____

_____

■ What more can I do to ensure that my team have sufficient opportunity to participate in planning a change?

_____

_____

_____

■ What more can I do to ensure that my team are always given the information, knowledge and skills they need to handle a particular change?

_____

_____

_____

2 Action plan

Use this plan to further develop for yourself a course of action you want to take. Make a note in the left-hand column of the issues or problems you want to tackle, and then decide what you want to do, and make a note in column 2.

The resources you need might include time, materials, information or money. You may need to negotiate for some of them, but others could be easy to acquired, like half an hour of somebody's time, or a chapter of a book. Put whatever you need in column 3. No plan means anything without a timescale, so put a realistic target completion date in column 4.

Finally, describe the outcome you want to achieve as a result of this plan, whether it is for your own benefit or advancement, or a more efficient way of doing things.

Desired outcomes			
1 Issues	2 Action	3 Resources	4 Target completion
Actual outcomes			

3 Extensions

Extension I

Book   *The Change Masters*
Author   Rosabeth Moss Kanter
Edition   1985
Publisher   Touchstone Books

This book is one of the great classics on the ability of organizations to change and how people respond.

Extension 2

Book   *Handbook for Creative Team Leaders*
Author   Tudor Rickards and Susan Moger
Edition   1999
Publisher   Gower

This book serves as a useful guide to leading teams through the process of creative improvement and change.

Extension 3

Book   *Essential Managers 12: Managing Change*
Author   Robert Heller
Edition   1998
Publisher   Dorling Kindersley

An easy-to-read overview of the many aspects of change in organizations is provided by this book.

These extensions can be taken up via your ILM Centre. They will either have them or will arrange for you to have access to them. However, it may be more convenient to check out the materials with your human resources people at work – they may well give you access. There are other good reasons for approaching your own people, for example they will become aware of your interest and you can involve them in your development.

4 Answers to self-assessment questions

Self-assessment 1 on pages 24–5

1 PESTLE stands for:

 c Political, Economic, Social, Technological, Legal and Environmental

2 a Pressures created by financial institutions, as well as governments and world events, contribute to **economic** factors.
 b **Social** factors may be long term or fleeting. Among the long-term factors are changes in the composition of the population.
 c The policies pursued by government help to shape **political** factors.
 d Consumer protection laws are among the **legal** factors.
 e Among **environmental** factors is the issue of finite resources.
 f Numerous inventions that have changed the way people work are among the **technological** factors.

3 Among an organization's **strengths** are the things it does well and the skills of its staff. Among an organization's **weaknesses** are the gaps in staff skills. **Threats** are those things in the environment that an organization must overcome. **Opportunities** are those things an organization should grasp if it is to develop and prosper.

4 You can keep up-to-date with developments that may affect your organization in the future by:

 ■ reading journals and newspapers;
 ■ talking to suppliers' representatives;
 ■ reading company newsletters and bulletins;
 ■ attending management briefings;
 ■ going on relevant courses;
 ■ talking to colleagues in other parts of the organization, and in other organizations.

5 The most correct statement is (b). Although concern about the environment imposes a variety of legal obligations on organizations, it also presents organizations with new ways of developing. They can, for example, make products with recyclable ingredients, or produce organic foods.

Self-assessment 2 on pages 42–3

1 The complete diagram of the continuous improvement cycle is as shown below.

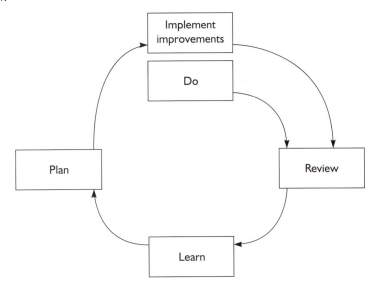

2 Providing quality products or services means meeting the **needs** of customers at **prices** they can afford. In today's competitive world, organizations should aim to actually exceed the **needs** of their customers. They can only do this through continuous improvement of their products and services, which in turn means continuous improvement of their **processes**. Continuous improvement results in constant **change.**

3 a Change can add interest to a job by getting you out of a tedious rut and re-awakening enthusiasm.
 b Change can mean new technology, new systems and a new role – and so it can give you the opportunity to learn new skills.
 c Change can provide an opportunity to give team members more control over what they do, but only if you, the team leader, are prepared to 'loosen the reins' and not stay totally in charge of everything.

4 a It is FALSE that all decisions are made at the top.
 b It is TRUE that suggestions for improvements to procedures are encouraged.
 c It is FALSE that there is a high level of conflict within and between teams.
 d It is TRUE that managers are generally considerate and supportive.

5 If a suggestion scheme is to be successful, you must not only acknowledge suggestions within 24 hours but evaluate them quickly, preferably within one week.

6 In order to maintain commitment among staff to continuous improvement you do not need:

 c Appraisal meetings with individual members of staff.

Self-assessment 3 on page 63

1 a Resistance to change is NORMAL.
   b People often resist change because of GENERAL UNCERTAINTY.
   c As a manager you should focus on how to respond to proposals for change in a CONSTRUCTIVE way.

2 Among the main underlying causes of people's resistance to change is that they see it as a threat to their position, prospects and **prosperity**.

3 You should aim to do both the following when faced with forces opposed to change.

   ■ Maintain the supporting forces at their present level.
   ■ Reduce the opposing forces.

4 a Where change is concerned, **participation** is the best antidote to resistance.
   b **Information** is the best medicine for uncertainty.
   c **Enthusiasm** is infectious.

5 Answers to the quick quiz

Answer 1   The six kinds of forces for change represented by the initials PESTLE are political, economic, social, technological, legal and environmental.

Answer 2   Among the environmental forces for change that have affected organizations in the last 30 years or so are the problems presented by pollution and finite resources. Among the effects of industrial pollution have been the depletion of the ozone layer and global warming, which in turn have led to laws banning the use of CFCs and imposing cuts in carbon dioxide emissions. Partly related to concerns over pollution is pressure, some of it legal, to increase the amount of recycling. The growing interest in organic food is also related to environmental concerns.

Answer 3   The initials SWOT stand for strengths, weaknesses, opportunities and threats.

Answer 4   In the cycle of continuous improvement, the next two steps after reviewing what has been done are learning from this review and planning improvements on the basis of what you have learned.

Answer 5   Among the positive aspects of change are that it can:

- bring new interest to a job;
- open up new prospects for career development;
- show a new slant on things;
- provide the opportunity to learn new skills;
- be a challenge;
- provide an opportunity to empower the team.

Answer 6   Among the features of a culture that is receptive to change are:

- friendly relations, based on mutual trust, within and between teams;
- generally considerate and supportive managers;
- decisions are made at all levels;
- there is scope for changing job roles;
- training is given whenever the need for new skills is identified;
- communication is two way and across levels, as well as up and down.
- staff are kept well informed;
- suggestions for improvements are encouraged;
- managers at all levels are encouraged to use initiative.

Answer 7   Suggestion schemes and quality circles are two methods for encouraging people to start coming up with ideas for change as part of a continuous improvement programme.

Answer 8   Among the techniques you can use in a meeting to get people to come up with ideas for improvements are brainstorming and building ideas.

Answer 9   There is no typical reaction to an unexpected job change: people react in different ways to different situations. However, it can be said to be quite 'normal' for change to be received with suspicion or hostility.

Answer 10   Among the methods that can be used by an organization to communicate everything staff need to know about a quality programme are circulars, regular emails, posters, newsletters, meetings, seminars and study days.

Answer 11   One possible answer to the question of how you would instil a feeling of ownership for planned change is to ensure that everyone:

- has the opportunity to participate in planning how the change is to be implemented;
- has the right information, knowledge and skills to handle the change.

Answer 12   In carrying out a force field analysis you identify the forces supporting change and the forces opposing change.

Answer 13   The letters PIE in the 'recipe' for overcoming resistance to change stand for participation, information and enthusiasm.

Answer 14   'Unfreezing' means reducing resistance towards change. 'Refreezing' is a word for the process whereby people become familiar with new ideas and new ways, and feel confident about them.

Answer 15   Among the suitable courses of action for you, as a team leader, in the refreezing stage are to:

- be receptive to feedback;
- be prepared to make adjustments to the original plan for change;
- seek the opinions of the workteam.

6 Certificate

Completion of the certificate by an authorized person shows that you have worked through all the parts of this workbook and satisfactorily completed the assessments. The certificate provides a record of what you have done that may be used for exemptions or as evidence of prior learning against other nationally certificated qualifications.

Pergamon Flexible Learning and ILM are always keen to refine and improve their products. One of the key sources of information to help this process is people who have just used the product. If you have any information or views, good or bad, please pass these on.

INSTITUTE OF LEADERSHIP & MANAGEMENT

SUPERSERIES

Understanding Change

....

has satisfactorily completed this workbook

Name of signatory ....

Position ....

Signature ....

Date ....

Official stamp

Fourth Edition

INSTITUTE OF LEADERSHIP & MANAGEMENT
SUPERSERIES
FOURTH EDITION

To order – phone us direct for prices and availability details (please quote ISBNs when ordering) on 01865 888190